LET'S TALK!

A Guide to Using Social Audio Apps to Succeed

NATASHA JORDAN

LET'S TALK

A Guide to Using Social Audio Apps to Succeed

Editing, formatting & cover design
RIA JAY Publishing
www.riajay.com

ISBN 979-8-9887614-3-3 (Paperback)
Printed in the United States of America
First printing August 2024

For additional copies, email us at:
Publishing@AllThingsNatashaJ.com
www.allthingsnatashaj.com

TABLE OF CONTENTS

INTRODUCTION

Social audio apps like Clubhouse, Twitter Spaces, Fanbase, and the newest social audio apps, Chatter, BeReal, Patreon, Substack, Mastodon, Locket, Tribel, CoHost, Hive Social, Yubo, Airchat, Counter Social, Polywork has taken the business world by storm. These live audio chat platforms offer invaluable networking and brand-building opportunities by bringing together engaged audiences eager to connect. However, effectively leveraging these apps to advance your career or business requires strategy and finesse.

The first key is approaching social audio networking with transparency, integrity, and purpose. Be clear about what unique value you bring and what you aim to gain. Establish yourself as a thought leader by sharing insights and experiences aligned with your brand. Making truthful connections based on mutual benefit paves the way for fruitful collaborations.

Grabbing attention and building community in these noisy virtual rooms is also essential. Have crisp self-promotional soundbites ready to distinguish yourself from the crowd.

Seek out affiliations and conversations with influencers in your field. Add value to discussions by asking insightful questions and making suggestions others find helpful. The goal is to leave a positive impression that energizes future working relationships.

While social audio apps can accelerate business success, you should set boundaries to avoid burnout. Be judicious in choosing which conversations to join rather than endlessly scrolling through rooms. Limit usage to focused time frames so it supplements other marketing efforts. Use these platforms' viral potential strategically rather than getting caught in an addictive cycle of chasing followers.

Approached purposefully and selectively, social audio networking heightens visibility and forges bonds that boost careers or brands. With proper self-regulation, the relationships cultivated can catalyze fruitful partnerships while democratizing access to key leaders. This introduction covers best practices to optimize results.

CHAPTER ONE

PREPARE YOURSELF

Successfully leveraging Clubhouse-like apps to advance professionally requires upfront self-examination. Before tapping into these platforms, clearly define your goals and the value you offer others. Be sure to inventory your existing online assets to showcase and share your expertise. When doing this, carefully consider what kinds of connections and outcomes you want to create. This self-knowledge and clarity of purpose allows for more intentional, fruitful networking. It also enables crafting a coherent personal brand story that builds credibility.

With defined intentions and self-awareness around your skills, advice to give, and support needed, social audio becomes less overwhelming and more strategically beneficial. The prep work is well worth it to maximize these apps' potential while minimizing wasted time and disappointing results. So, turn the microphone inward to find your voice before projecting it outward to grow your reach.

Be Transparent, Honest, Respectful, and Professional

Being transparent, honest, respectful, and professional is non-negotiable for succeeding on social audio networking platforms. In these voice-based forums, visibility is vulnerability—you articulate ideas in real-time without edit filters or deletion, exposing you to judgment of unseen audiences. The intimacy created from this mandates high integrity. Even minor duplicity detected in your messaging or behavior can permanently damage credibility and trust.

Start by ensuring complete alignment between how you portray yourself on social audio apps and in reality. Provide accurate background information and qualifications when relevant without embellishing achievements. Disclose boundaries of your expertise and acknowledge if you've made mistakes addressing specific topics. Such candor humanizes your brand, which in turn attracts listeners seeking genuine connections instead of flawless gurus.

Next, commit to truthful storytelling, sharing motivations, opinions, and experiences. Don't simply say what you think listeners want to hear. Authenticity resonates. And if specific personal details don't comfortably fit within your brand image, avoid rather than deceive. On these apps, transparency doesn't require full disclosure about your private life—just no false projection.

Interacting respectfully also proves critical, especially when disagreements emerge. Pause before replying to emotionally charged comments. This gives you time to respond thoughtfully, acknowledging valid points even when you dispute someone's position. Such judicious dialogue keeps conversations enlightening rather than alienating. It earns you admiration, not enemies.

Overall, you build social capital on any social audio platform by internalizing these values of forthrightness, consideration for others, and leading with integrity. Those seeking phoniness can find it elsewhere. You offer substance.

Identify your Purpose

Defining your purpose is essential before engaging extensively on social audio platforms. This exercise brings intentional clarity so networking conversations align with advancing your goals, not just aimless chatter. Be specific in what brings you to these apps so your self-articulated motivations guide your participation.

Start by clarifying what you want to achieve in the near and longer-term future by leveraging this access to audiences. Are you aiming to drive product sales? Spread awareness about your creative talents or business services? Seeking collaborators for an upcoming project? Wish to impact your field by sharing insights? Know whether you're focused on commercial outcomes or influencing change.

Next, reflect on your unique value that would compel others to help you achieve the above aims through their follows, shares, and positive word-of-mouth. Take inventory of signature strengths and knowledge from your experiences. Get comfortable summarizing into a compelling brand story underscoring why audiences should care about your offerings.

Also, outline what types of listeners you want to connect with and support your goals. What are your dream mentors? Partners? Early adopters of what you sell? Typical demographic profile? Subject matter enthusiasts? Outlining your ideal community helps you pursue relevant conversations.

Revisiting this sense of purpose centers you when navigating busy social audio spaces swarming with distractions. It helps qualify where to spend time meaningfully and who merits further nurturing of a relationship. When your internal compass guides external interactions, you network efficiently and impactfully. Your raison d'être focuses on conversations, so listening ears become amplifiers for your success.

CHAPTER TWO

BUILD YOUR BRAND

Successfully leveraging social audio's networking potential requires having a professional brand presence ready to showcase. Before promoting your business or talents on these vocal platforms, ensure you have digital assets actively demonstrating your expertise. Curate an aesthetically pleasing, up-to-date website highlighting past work and achievements. Populate social media with rich content that engages followers. The more substantive your online footprint appears, the more credible a voice you'll have in networking conversations.

Be prepared to communicate what you offer listeners succinctly, then direct them to online properties that compel further discovery. You'll inspire new supporters with a foundation built to validate your vocal pitches visually. So, do the legwork to develop an exemplary brand experience beyond the audio-only apps. That way, whatever vision for yourself you share verbally can be quickly confirmed visually.

Be Ready to Explain Your Brand

Being ready to explain your brand clearly in social audio forums is a prerequisite to effective networking. It helps to have an eloquent self-definition prepared that summarizes who you are, what you offer, and why audiences should care. This crisp verbal brand narrative builds future alliance and convinces listeners that you merit memorability.

Start by distilling the essence of your professional identity into a succinct descriptive tagline. For example, "Empowering small business owners through digital marketing strategy" or "Architect of elegantly functional web design." Such positioning statements quickly communicate your value.

Next, have a 30-second brand "origin story" ready to paint an impactful picture of why you are passionate about your work. Share what excites you in problem-solving for customers or how previous experiences shaped your commitment to excellence. Even a snippet of your journey gets others invested.

Also, prepare examples of signature services and products, top achievements you're proud of, and testimonials from happy clients describing your impact. Such social proof builds authority. And have a list of brand differentiators handy — what makes your offerings distinct that breeds loyal customers? Broadcast standout attributes.

Lastly, spell out precisely what you want listeners who resonate with your brand to do next, whether to follow you on other platforms, visit your website, or set up exploratory meetings. Strong calls to action turn impressions into concrete connections.

With these brand communication tools sharpened — succinct tagline, backstory, bragging rights, testimonials, and explicit requests — you can compellingly convey what makes you and your services recognizable and memorable in any social audio room. You become primed for productive networking.

Have Sales Materials Prepared

Having polished sales materials ready to share is vital for converting social audio app connections into business. Casual networking conversations plant seeds of interest in what you offer, but you need prepared assets to drive prospects to act by purchasing your product or service. Think through an ecosystem that supports vocal pitches with visual presentation.

An elegant, informative website is the cornerstone, showcasing offerings for browsers post-chats to check you out. Ensure pages eloquently communicate value with easy purchasing functionality or built-in contact forms. Upload videos demonstrating your expertise in action. Refresh blogs regularly with insider advice central to your niche, optimizing discoverability.

Prepare downloadable one-pagers with services and pricing to email on request. Craft exclusive lead magnets like checklists, toolkits, or guidebooks in exchange for contacts information. Automate email sequences to nurture prospects and create re-marketing display ads to engage newcomers.

In addition, leverage broader social channels like Instagram or LinkedIn to reinforce credibility. Utilize Twitter to share blog article links to drive traffic. Curate highlight reels on YouTube or Spotify that exhibit your skills. Sync messaging.

With this sales apparatus working behind the scenes, casual networking chats generate captured contacts and concrete opportunities. So, develop the ecosystem to channel vocal vibes into returns beyond the soundstage. What begins as ephemeral audio impressions becomes actual world revenue through prepared promotion materials that deliver.

➢ Website:

A polished website is the pillar around which successful social audio networking revolves, converting new contacts into customers. When crafting the website, visitors will learn from app conversations to be highly intentional about aesthetic design and content strategy. Your site's look should align with your brand identity. Choose visually pleasing yet professional color schemes, font pairings, and balanced use of negative space so navigation is straightforward. Ensure visual assets like product photography or creator headshots are of professional quality, each element reinforcing your market positioning. A cohesive user interface that thoughtfully guides visitors to take action conveys competence - because first impressions influence conversions.

Regarding on-site copy, display concise yet compelling information of the most vital value propositions you offer within above-the-fold sections to spark interest quickly before scrolling deeper. Quantify past successes via testimonials or critical metrics like "500+ satisfied members." Share insider tips and tricks that reveal expertise. Insert a short video welcome message to humanize the brand. Outline logical next steps via a fixed footer CTA guiding visitors to purchase, schedule appointments, or subscribe for updates. Integrate email sign-up forms seamlessly into a sidebar or blog post footer. This seamlessly optimizes opt-in incentivizes and gain potential leads gathered from far-flung social audio network referrals, repaying your networking time investments. The website sets each guest's relationship with your business on a trajectory towards lifetime value. So, perfecting its commercial impact and aesthetic quality elevates the whole operation's potential.

➢ Social Media:

A savvy social media presence sets the stage for social audio app networking to thrive by pre-seeding brand familiarity and goodwill.

Curate Instagram and LinkedIn accounts to visually intrigue professional peers before conversations convert strangers into website visitors.

On Instagram, lean into aesthetically pleasing imagery that communicates core values. Showcase team members in authentic moments that humanize your business. If selling physical products, photoshoot them artfully styled complementary products that inspire customers. For service providers, consider effective before-and-after style transformations conveying uplifting results. Share user-generated content from delighted clients proud to rave about working with you. Ask followers questions in Stories and re-post responses to validate engagement.

LinkedIn requires a more knowledge-centered, edge appropriate approach to its career-minded audience. Position founders and top talent linked to long-form biodata detailing areas of specialty. Share varied educational, inspirational, or promotional updates according to the buyer's journey stage. Added value industry advice builds subject authority, while press mentions signal external validation. Stay top-of-mind by commenting on strategic new connections' updates.

With tailored strategies humanizing the brand, social channels become lead-generating launch pads once social audio conversations convert interested strangers into followers. These platforms should spotlight strengths before directing visitors to transact through the website. Consistent messaging strengthens credibility, so network-ing feels like engaging with an old friend vs. just hype from an un-known entity. The visual seeds planted multiply networking returns.

➤ Sales pitch:

An irresistible sales pitch is the make-or-break tool for converting social audio conversations into business. Before networking, step back and analyze the customer journey to deeply understand the pain points your offerings solve. Listen to past client testimonials identi-fying the most significant challenges you alleviated. Uncover the psychological transformation that happens once customers enjoy life benefiting from your solution. Define this in emotional, human-centered language that resonates. Lead by naming the anxiety, frus-tration, or limitations most desperately wanting resolution rather than jumping to product features. This framing showcases empathy.

Next, spotlight the signature strengths you uniquely possess to de-liver results, your "special sauce." Whether years perfecting tech-nical mastery, holistic process, exceptional responsiveness, or pre-mium materials - tell differentiated stories. Quantify achievements through compelling metrics like "increased productivity 32%" or "500 five-star reviews". Vivid specificity sells credibility, so you feel like their needs are answered on a silver platter.

Lastly, address pricing transparency head-on to reduce potential sticker shock. Explain the immense value customers receive for investments in your superior solution. Give real examples of transformations - before inefficiencies costing hidden time/money like $5000 monthly...after optimizing operations via you for just a $500 monthly fee. Compare severe pains without you with life-improving by partnering with you.

This human-centered positioning, differential comparison, and value pricing form sales pitches that prompt invested listeners to ask, "What's next?! How can I learn more or buy NOW?" Seed these conversational fruits-harvesting contact info to nurture towards purchase. Masterful pitches sow persuasion.

➢ Lead users off the app to purchase:

Capitalizing on networking's contact gathering requires prepared sales funnels that deliberately convert new leads into first purchases. Guide interested contacts to opt-in landing pages by providing enticing tripwire deals for more visibility into your offerings. For example, build valuable info products like how-to video courses, curated resource libraries, or rich assessments delivering personalized advice unlockable through email subscription. Make accessing your know-how irresistible.

Then, nurture subscribers via messages sequenced to mirror the customer journey. Early on, prioritize educational value-sharing advice and community over constant product promotion. Branch conversations by interest based on assessment results or downloaded materials. When the time is right, offer exclusive discounts or payment plan options to incentivize trial commitments.

Keep visibility high between messages with remarketing campaigns, including social media ads, retargeting website display ads, and online community forum sponsorships. Set the license term that if a contact goes a designated number of days without experiencing your brand's value since downloading a resource, automatically remind them.

Overall, post-purchase, the goal is to enrich every customer's experience and fulfill unmet needs. But at the initial conversion phase, escort interested contacts down a journey with multiple on-ramps to saying "yes" to that first transaction. Meet them where hesitations arise with content that clarifies. Structure payment plans for scaled commitment. Have sales materials ready for every "almost" lead until deals close.

CHAPTER THREE

IDENTIFY & ENGAGE
YOUR AUDIENCE

S uccessfully connecting with potential clients on social audio apps requires strategic audience targeting. Rather than randomly sampling busy forums, thoughtfully identify rooms rich with your best-fit prospects based on clearly defined ideal customer attributes. Leverage search tools scoping discussion topics and community demographics to pinpoint aligned niches. Invest preparation time researching relevant voices with strong visibility that are worth engaging. Have icebreakers ready to position your value, add if chat flow permits. Personalize networking outreach to stand out amidst the noise. With purposeful targeting, listening first to integrate offerings and customized pitches contextually, you can transform transient audio encounters into meaningful business relationships through authentic engagement that resonates. The profits lie in selective, savvy audience pursuit.

Figure Out Where Your Potential Clients Are

Pinpointing where your ideal customers congregate on social audio apps is step one for efficient networking. Rather than guessing, leverage research tools to identify targeted demographics and discussions aligned to your business niche.

Many apps organize rooms by categories, featured speakers, or group topics, so browse strategically. Follow hashtags reflecting your specialty. Look for surging, popular forums versus stagnant ones. Investigate intersecting communities speaking to significant subcultures or challenges prime for your solutions. Study scheduled event listings for industry conferences, founder town halls, and VIP Q&A's attracting influential product users. Invest time exploring trending room rosters and membership lists for priority communities aligned to your buyer personas.

Approach connections with exploratory, not salesy questions, to source referrals to their quality communities of choice. Over time, you can curate a customized dashboard of go-to rooms for each niche.

Thoughtful prospecting research, referrals, and in-app exploration reveal ideal hot spots for engaging potential clients tuned into topics and challenges you solve. Show consistently in the right conversations instead of spraying irrelevant spaces, and your networking productivity will skyrocket.

Engage with Them Immediately

Capitalizing on social audio's networking potential means actively engaging new contacts with personalized outreach immediately after promising conversations. In these fleeting verbal forums where voices fade quickly into the ether, swift follow-up cement connections, showing you prioritize promising partners.

Start by directly requesting new additions during or after productive chats to broaden your circle of visibility. Capture contact details verbally offered to coordinate off-app. Then, bring up your social media handles or website to allow interested participants to connect via channels where your brand presence and work portfolio live on full display.

Next, send direct messages post-chat, recapping enjoyable dialogue highlights while personally introducing yourself. Include links to helpful resources mentioned that listeners requested more details about. Ask thoughtful questions about current initiatives they're focused on. Offer your availability to continue helpful discussions by phone if relevant.

Also, schedule time on your calendar shortly after meeting new VIPs to craft thoughtfully customized connection requests on their platform profiles referencing what resonated. Compliment admiral qualities in the chat that distinguishes them as someone you're eager to engage moving forward.

Through personalized communication, the key is demonstrating genuine interest in their identity beyond surface-level small talk. Ask how you can contribute to their current business challenges with relevant expertise. Explore shared passions for collaborating. Deliver praise and resources and follow up promptly.

By initiating ongoing, value-added communication, you stand out from the crowds flooding new contacts' inboxes with autoresponder promotions. Deepening nascent relationships via purposeful engagement pays dividends.

Stand Out in a Room of Strangers

Standing out as an authoritative expert within busy social audio rooms full of strangers requires strategic positioning. Rather than aggressive self-promotion, your goal is graciously capturing attention. This involves showcasing personality and insights that intrigue.

Start by crafting interesting icebreaker introductions when rooms invite new members to chime in. Share your name, location, and niche focus, then sprinkle in unexpected personal tidbits that humanize you. Maybe highlight an unusual hobby, favorite book genre, or specialty food you're passionate about. Such flavor builds memorable first impressions.

Next, as the conversation unfolds, analyze room temperature before asserting vocal presence again. Discern patterns in who moderators call on most or subjects receiving high engagement. Lean into topics connected to your expertise, but ensure suggestions align with flow.

When contributing, raise fresh angles on recurring issues or pose thought-provoking questions rather than just stating opinions. Offer relevant case studies and actionable advice while acknowledging others' contributions first. This educational authority earns listening ears without arrogance.

You can also volunteer to present specially prepared mini-trainings on your niche or moderate discussions on high-demand subjects. Position supporting quotes, stats, and anecdotes to slot seamlessly into many contexts. Soon, your unique blend of friendliness, wisdom, and helpfulness causes members to tune in, anticipating what you'll say.

With consistency, constructive participation, and not centering every comment on self, your vocal brand reshapes strangers' perspectives so they lean into your leadership. The room reads your value. Thus, curiosity builds around the expertise you spotlight in service of collective growth.

Give Extensive Explanation on This

The fastest way to grow on social audio platforms is strategically aligning with influential creators already commanding large, loyal followings in your niche. Rather than starting from scratch, identify widely respected thought leaders and trailblazers to collaborate with expanding your shared voice.

Start by researching relevant hashtags and browsing suggested user lists for noted bestselling authors, five-star rated podcasters, award-winning bloggers, and industry pioneers flagged as experts by media and conferences.

Look for creators enthusiastically recommended when members ask others' favorite people to follow. Notice who hosts the most popular recurring rooms or events, drawing engaged crowds. Their flock likely signals an aligned audience.

Contact shortlisted standouts via DM describing shared values and audience overlap you identified. Offer customized ideas for delivering their followers amplified value through collaborative initiatives like co-hosted talks, cross-podcast interviews, co-created downloadable guides, or other joint content showcasing complementary strengths.

Also, explore endorsing their offerings to your current following, if substantial, through announcements in your letter or affiliate promotions spreading the word of their work. Public praise for talents you admire organically builds reciprocal goodwill.

Ideally, brainstorm evergreen partnerships beyond one-off appearances. Entwine communities through lead sharing or product bundling. Partnered creators combining follower bases gain collective credibility and expanded visibility neither could achieve alone. So, pool strengths for exponential impact through ongoing support.

Keep a List of Potential Partners/Clients Ready to Reference

Curating a go-to list of high-potential partners and clients to connect with on social audio apps ensures your networking efforts stay focused on nurturing priority relationships versus getting distracted chatting with peripheral players.

Start by auditing your current customer roster and identifying common positive attributes of favorite clients to work with, such as fast payment, high lifetime value, influencers providing testimonials, or critical network connectors opening doors. Note what distinguishes delightful partners so you can deliberately seek more ideal matches with scale.

Also, reflect on past collaborators who enhanced the quality of your work through complementary skills like stunning graphic designers, nimble software coders, and subject matter experts lending thought leadership. Outline beneficial roles you'd welcome in your alliance circle.

Conduct field research, visiting industry discussions, and influencer spaces aligned to your offerings. Scout standout contributors who exhibit domains of expertise, leadership qualities, or community connections that could amplify your shared efforts if combined.

Track these high-potential partners and clients in a master list with notes about their offerings, relevant social profiles, and conversation details for future personalized outreach reminders. Having this qualified roster minimizes time wasted chatting up dead ends.

Revisit and expand this VIP list often as you encounter exciting new protagonists. Add tags and group similar targets into buckets for future initiatives like podcast interviews, access to lucrative referrals, or prospective passionate affiliate partners.

Staying focused on your North Star prospects guides social audio networking toward building a mighty circle of collaborative advocates, not just transient talkers.

Have Icebreaker Intro Questions Ready

Crafting a shortlist of go-to icebreaker questions is essential for instantly assessing room receptivity while showcasing the value you offer fellow members. Rather than generically stating basics like name and location when introduced, spark intrigue by blending personable rapport building with strategic positioning.

Have a standard opener ready such as, "Thanks for having me! I'm [name] tuning in from [city], where I help [niche] leverage [offering] to tackle [common frustration]. You can find me [interesting hobby/quirk] when I'm not empowering clients. So fun to join you all! What initially drew you to this discussion?" This formula blends approachability with professional credentials so strangers perceive you as an accessible expert.

Prepare other openers tailored to frequently attended room topics that describe helpful solutions you provide. "Glad to join this growth strategy chat! As someone who supports female founders scaling smoothly, I'm excited to hear what scaling hurdles you are currently facing. My agency tackles operational bottlenecks, funding gaps, and leadership development. What growth barriers feel hardest to tackle alone right now as we map advice?"

Adapt questions based on moderators' prompts, like "If you could instantly gain one superpower to multiply the growth of your business overnight, what would you choose and why?" This invites playful responses that still reveal ideal partnerships.

Having a stack of icebreakers that fluidly introduce your brand's value while learning about fellow leaders' needs builds instant connection. You gather intel assessing fit while spotlighting goodwill chemistry.

Offer Insights Early on

The key to establishing credible vocal authority in social audio rooms is strategically offering value-added insights before mentioning your offerings early on. Listen closely as conversations unfold to pinpoint unmet needs or knowledge gaps limiting members' decision-making. Then, make your first contributions around ask-provoking observations, constructive ideas, and helpful resources to empower fellow users versus self-promotion.

For example, if members debate the pros and cons of various software platforms for streamlining operations, chime in: "Great cost comparison on those options! As the owner of an automation consultancy, the biggest pitfall I've seen is tools promising the world while lacking sufficient customer support post-purchase when learning curves hit. I'd be curious: Which providers have you seen best educate users beyond initial demos? My agency offers implementation blueprints for the top 3 tools mentioned here to offset that disconnect if anyone wants added input."

This showcases niche expertise while building reciprocity and generosity, defining your brand before requesting follow-ups. A place giving value higher priority over taking value in these intro exchanges until you earn engagement through wisdom.

You can also weave in data like fresh statistics published validating famous hunches members propose or examples of creative applications from adjacent industries they may lack visibility into. Sprinkle listening sessions with little "Did you know?" showcasing what your insider lens reveals before you ever advertise services. Offer help and intrigue before the hard sell.

Personalize Outreach when Requesting Profile Connections

Making meaningful connections on networking apps means personalizing outreach versus sending generic invites en masse to bolster numbers. I thoughtfully customize requests referencing details that resonate from conversations as signals that this relationship matters.

Start connection by noting specific rooms where you enjoyed interacting or praiseworthy insights the member contributed that stood out. Quote a joke that made you laugh or a memorable metaphor they used explaining challenges. Reference any follow-up links promised or describe helpful takeaways gained from their wisdom or stories.

Weave in genuine compliments praising admirable qualities exhibited in discussions like grace facilitating debates, courage to challenge assumptions, emotional IQ supporting members, or creative problem-solving. Such praise for their fine personhood, not just business function, uplifts.

Ask questions based on intel gathered about current initiatives they're tackling where you may offer relevant guidance from parallel experiences. Offer your availability for further exchanges and continuing helpful dialogue threads.

Finally, explain quickly why aligning could offer mutual value, not just vague networking banalities. For example, note overlapping audience niches perfect for cross-collaboration and complementary skill sets worthwhile to brainstorm around or introductions to needed partners you could facilitate. Articulate purpose.

Specificity is the antidote to superficial outreach volume. Detail-laden engagement requests demonstrate genuine goodwill, not copy-pasted platitudes. So, personalize invites as the first stitch knitting truly supportive professional bonds, not just contact list padding from strangers soon forgotten.

CHAPTER FOUR

TRANSACT BUSINESS

Effectively transacting business on social audio platforms requires strategic stage-setting before public conversations and intentional follow-up once connections signify sales-readiness. Ensure your vocal promotion and digital sales infrastructure align with terms of service by directing interested prospects off-platform to formalize purchases. Tactfully transition from deal identification to negotiated proposals through personalized channels like email or messengers. Prepare to showcase products, pricing, and testimonials in a compliant way that continues to build rapport socially. The art of closing sales seeded in these apps lies not in public transactions where communities gather but in afterglow customer care crafting deals. Masterfully steward contacts onward with integrity.

Close Deals on the App

While social audio apps offer unparalleled relationship-building potential through vocal chat engagements, directly closing business deals should strategically occur off-platform to avoid breaching terms of service. Savvy networkers thoughtfully transition promising prospects into more formalized purchasing settings conducive to transaction specifics.

You can nurture connections initiated in rooms by suggestively name-dropping products and services as natural chatter, which allows for solution brainstorming. Tactfully say, "I may have additional thoughts on optimizing so we could explore 1-on-1 offline later." This plant intends to be sales.

Then, follow up through email or messenger to reference aspects discussed and continue the helpful dialogue in a private environment, which is ownable long term, not just temporary public chats. "Great trading notes on common video production roadblocks in the Clubhouse earlier. I wanted to expand insights on cost-saving studio builder hacks we briefly mentioned that my agency leverages. When might you have 30 minutes this week for a quick call? I have a case study on tripling quality while lowering spend I'd love to overview."

Now guided to personalized communication channels, vividly display portfolio samples, pricing documents, payment integration abilities, or testimonials that advance the prospect relationship while answering outstanding questions. Listen for verbal buying signals like budget parameters and feature priorities.

Once interest feels entirely mutual, officially propose business terms by email or document, negotiated until alignment is reached. Then, smoothly facilitate contract finalization and payment portal access to complete the customer journey.

Thoughtful verbal engagement, strategic off-platform follow-up while showcasing capabilities, and facilitation contracting once buyers signal ready allow proper stewarding of app connections to sales conversions without misconduct. Stick to site guidelines but skillfully progress relationships onward.

Make Sure Potential Clients Are Trustworthy

Vetting the credibility of prospective clients encountered through social audio networking before formalizing business relationships or sharing vulnerable information is crucial protection. While forging connections feels exciting in these vocal forums, remain objective. Scan profiles, search names, and politely probe references to verify legitimacy before investing in collaborations, not just chatter.

Start by glancing at pinned links and bios for any obvious red flags like missing professional details commonplace on standard accounts. Cross-reference names on other networks, viewing engagement metrics and history breadcrumbs to assess authenticity. Probe their supposed expertise by asking thoughtful clarification questions as conversations unfold.

Specifically, request they expand on client case studies, development of flagship offerings, and origin stories founding their company. Keep the tone curious, not interrogatory, while assessing if narratives align and impress.

Gauge receptivity suggests a reference call with 1-2 past partners who could vouch for positive experiences. Or ask if they have published media features or speaking appearances documenting achievements you could review before formalizing the association.

Essentially, seek organic proof points qualifying their trustworthiness through actions, not just vocal claims alone. If hesitant to supply verification, leverage search tools like social media listening, domain registry lookups, and credential confirmation databases to fact-check.

While social audio interactions feel intimate given voice connections, remember unseen identities operate behind curated auditory personas. So, verify, qualify, and authenticate potential partners through layered insights before sharing your hard-won authority with unvalidated players. Not all vocal chemistry converts to credible collaborations, so strategically vet.

Discuss Best Practices for Transitioning from Deal Identification to Formalized Purchasing Offline

Capitalizing on the customer connections made by socializing in audio rooms requires strategic stewardship, formalizing interest into sales. While apps rightfully limit overt public transactions, you can nurture introduced leads toward finalized purchasing done ethically offline or via direct communication channels.

Start conversations by casually name-dropping existing offerings relevant to challenges voiced in the group, avoiding spammy pitches. Tactfully say, "That reminds me of customizable solutions my company has guided other firms to implement, addressing the frustrations you raised..." Plant ideas, then discuss with other members to keep the tone natural.

After sparking initial interest, follow up post-chat to continue the helpful dialogue in a private, ownable environment, not just temporary rooms. Warmly reference aspects they previously found useful, then interject additional assets they requested to pursue the next step, self-education.

"I'm following up on the positioning strategy exchange on Tuesday. Since many found the statistics around social media ROI use cases helpful, I wanted to pass along the advanced metrics guide my agency gives clients detailing ideal benchmarking tailored to business model and budget. Do you have 10 minutes to overview the approach on a call this Friday briefly?"

In personalized engagement, fully display case studies, demos, and testimonials that alleviate outstanding concerns while quantifying your track record of success specifically relevant to their needs.

Once verbal buying signals occur, like budget approval to access your offerings, officially submit polished proposals outlined in the terms via email.

Facilitate seamless transition through contracting, payment finalization, and onboarding until the conversion is completed. Shephard social connections secured on audio apps into satisfied customers through compliant, post-chat courtship.

Partner with Aligned Creators on Virtual Events Combining Communities

Strategically partnering with aligned creators to assemble virtual events, summits, or conferences that combine both communities' audiences can immensely expand collective reach. Identify influencers already commanding loyalty among niche demographics similar to your followers. Then, co-design digital programming featuring your varied perspectives on shared topics that fans value.

For example, an interior designer and real estate investor serving aspiring homeowners could host a digital summit on "Preparing Your Dream Home: Design + Finance Keys." Each could moderate separate panel discussions in their specialty or co-facilitate a joint session blending guidance.

Similarly, a dating coach and image consultant supporting single professionals could organize a virtual tour stop on "Finding the One:

Confidence from Dating to Fashion." Attendees would gain well-rounded wisdom from these complementary experts.

A healthcare journalist and medical inventor may partner on a virtual festival, helping patients advocate their needs with clinicians, uniting innovation insights alongside patient experience advice.

Promoting collaborator events multiplies exposure beyond just sole creator visibility. It also incentivizes fans of one expert to expand perspectives engaging with the collaborating voice's community. Well-matched co-productions introduce new followers.

Explore Brand Collaborations with Companies Reaching Shared Audiences

Exploring win-win brand collaborations with companies reaching similar target audiences allows for effectively expanding collective visibility and offerings. Identify likely partners with complementary solutions but non-competing product lines primed for strategic alignment. Analyze where consumer overlap exists between loyal followers. Then, co-create expanded experiences benefiting shared accounts through coordinated cross-promotion.

For example, an eco-friendly skincare startup selling plant-based lotions could collaborate with a niche organic cotton apparel brand on a limited-edition branded self-care box for Earth Day featuring jointly created products. Each promotes on their e-newsletters, social media, and influencer networks. Shared values win consumers while expanding impressions.

Similarly, a virtual productivity coach may collaborate with time-tracking software developers on an exclusive goal-setting workshop and tool bundle aimed explicitly at aiding entrepreneurs. Cross-sells incentivize the coaching community to adopt helpful new systems and vice versa.

Even a fitness trainer could partner with a niche sports equipment manufacturer on a giveaway for specialized product testing in training classes. User reviews and social content generated from this partnership will fuel both companies' organic reach and research.

Seeking mission-aligned yet non-directly competitive partners to brainstorm experiences serving each audience amplifies exposure for both brands cost-effectively while letting collaboration partners shoulder some marketing efforts in service of mutually constructive goals. So, explore creative pairings!

Barter Services with Top Creators

Savvy social audio networkers strategically partner with top creators to exchange value, amplifying each other's visibility and credibility via bartered contributions instead of paid promotions. Identify voices with synergistic brand alignment and strong embedded authority among their loyal following. Then brainstorm collaborative content, community enrichment and lead sharing arrangements benefiting both parties.

For example, an elegant jewelry designer might offer product placement mailings to a fashion blogger's most engaged first-tier list subscribers which that influencer normally charges for. In return the blogger can provide quotes and imagery the designer leverages across packaging and websites as social proof.

A photography coach might guest-moderate a recurring Clubhouse room for a leading podcaster in return for multimedia branding assets like professional headshots and video highlight reels amplified across that broadcaster's social channels.

Two startup founders serving similar demographics can choose to co-author a trend report or cross-promote respective online courses bundling offerings for added buyer incentive while expanding reach.

Proposing value exchanges without direct payment builds goodwill and lasting reciprocal gain. Bartered arrangements lend founders bonus credibility as curators, handpicking partners worthy of vouching for rather than random sponsors paying for vanity associations. So collaboratively elevating each other earns authentic authority.

CHAPTER FIVE

SET BOUNDARIES

Establishing healthy boundaries for social audio engagement pays dividends in efficiency and morale. Without self-regulation of these voice chat mediums that trigger dopamine hits from always-on notifications re-engaging you, networking participation can spiral unconstructively. Set automatic time limits for guard railing usage daily and weekly. Temper's external app triggers constantly breaking focus with inner wisdom guiding intentional participation aligned to conversion goals, not just crowd approval. Audit ROI regularly, assessing if conversions justify the schedule invested or if shifting approach improves outcomes. Boundaries breed value-driven actions, not endless distractions in these infinitely fascinating forums. Wield self-discipline as the compass guiding this journey, outwardly expanding connections while inwardly centering your best interests first. From that, solid foundation flows networking that amplifies your purpose.

Don't Drain Yourself Mentally or Physically.

While social audio networking provides unparalleled connection opportunities, managing participation time wisely prevents mental or physical burnout. Set firm daily and weekly limits guarding against addictively long sessions straining voice and attention. Schedule mandatory offline breaks to refuel between stretching, hydrating, and walking outdoors. Temper's constant app re-engagement is triggered by distracting notifications and fear of missing out. Instead, participate intentionally for just 1-2 critical hours daily aligned to energy peaks when feeling sharpest. No more powering through fatigue chasing crowd approval highs. Preserve that finite currency for just results-focused efforts.

Beyond scheduling guardrails, assess if current approaches lead to disproportionate energy expenditure versus deal profits generated. If overly taxing tactics deplete morale without sufficient conversion return on time invested, rework strategies. For example, transition overwhelming cold outreach to vetting warmer referral intros first. Swap long listening roadshows across random rooms for 3-5 tailored community touchpoints where your best buyers gather. Not all networking time equally rewards, so correct what drains versus fuels.

Overall, nurture almost sacred respect for the precious non-renewable resource of your mind, voice, and nervous system, always requiring protective stewardship before institutional platform growth goals. Set networking participation limits aligned to your human needs first. Sustainable success through social audio apps ironically requires extraordinary offline analog life boundaries so the digital extensions can thrive without eclipsing your whole being. The inner compass pointing towards actual north well-being guides external usage, too.

Set Limits on Your Daily Usage

Establishing prudent time limits for daily social audio usage preserves energy and effectiveness rather than endlessly browsing ephemeral conversations chasing dopamine engagement highs. Define how long each session's purpose serves so voices and attention don't become fatigued.

Start by auditing your calendar and typical peak performance rhythms. Which 60-90-minute window aligns best with your ideological sharpness and verbal stamina for networking? Morning thinkers should connect then. Night owls claim evening hours. Block your beneficial slot as sacrosanct for just voice chat relationship building and follow-up correspondence.

Now, surround sessions with 30-60 minutes of buffers before and after for winding up and down transition rituals. Connect offline beforehand to gather thoughts or review prep notes so the time feels focused. Then, post-chat, immediately download takeaways while ideas feel fresh before processing insights the next working day.

Avoid endless aimless participation once your designated social audio hours conclude each day. Turn off the non-essential app alerts that tempt return visits outside your block. Schedule preferred activities shifting gears like family meals or exercise. Establish closing rituals indicating that the segment of focus is wrapped.

Setting intentional limits on networking participation aligned to human energy patterns liberates the rest of your days for higher priority work and complete rest without persistent voice chat intrusions. Define and defend beneficial boundaries so these platforms expand but don't overwhelm daily life. Discipline, when desiring distraction, determines destiny.

Time Limit Networking and Follow-up Sessions Daily

Optimizing social audio networking productivity involves thoughtfully segmenting participation into distinct networking and follow-up phases timed appropriately. This structured approach ensures conversations directly generate captured value, not just fleeting enjoyment alone.

First, explicitly schedule no more than 1-2 hours maximum daily for popping into relevant industry discussion rooms, panels, or mixers. Arrive prepared to introduce offerings where helpful or take notes on promising contacts met. But brevity prevents vocal strain and decision fatigue. Wrap visiting rounds when energy remains high, exiting before mental clarity wavers.

Then, directly allocate 30-60 minutes daily to follow-up correspondence. Review recordings or notes from the earlier sessions. Quickly craft customized connection requests to promising new members referencing specific engaging exchanges. Attach any links, case studies, or resources potentially enriching budding relationships.

Importantly, also connect via email or messaging to thank moderators and recap helpful advice received. Offer your availability for continuing dialogue by phone if they have the capacity. Demonstrate genuine, personalized investment into these new ties.

Segmenting structured networking blocks followed by priority relationship stewardship times compels promptly capturing value from conversations before recall fades. It builds habitual value extraction rhythms after transient but inspiring live interactions. Timebound phases prevent potential allies from forgetfulness. Be present socially and then privately progress relationships through consistent segmented daily effort, not just public performance.

Avoid Constant Intrusive Notifications

While social audio apps rely on trigger notifications to continually re-engage users, managing these persistent alerts judiciously prevents distractions from tanking productivity. Temper external triggers with internal wisdom on beneficial participation boundaries.

Start by turning off non-essential notification badges, sounds, and frequency. Restrict alerts only from priority individuals, groups, or event RSVPs you follow. Mute channels when temporarily needing no disturbances for deep work.

Also, consciously disengage from anxiety around missing out if stepping away briefly. Remind yourself live rooms still exist on replay, and critical conversations will be referenced again. The world will wait.

Wield power to intentionally exit apps for increasing intervals without continuously refreshing for the sake of novelty. Gradually strengthen psychological immunity to FOMO when important tasks require full attention elsewhere.

Essentially, take back authority over technology compulsion rather than letting design hooks push endless engagement. Set app parameters and notifications strictly serving your human needs first - not platform growth or surface-level socializing.

With empowered self-regulation, you control these tools in service of conversational commerce and community enrichment goals in balanced proportion without losing days to diffuse distraction. Set boundaries, and focus follows.

Regularly Assess if Conversions are Justifying Time Invested

Optimizing social media networking requires regularly auditing performance data to assess whether direct business conversions justify the calendar hours invested or if strategy adjustments may improve ROI.

Start by tracking key metrics like total new followers, profile views, and connection requests garnered weekly from social audio apps specifically. Note which discussions, groups, or partnerships drive the most visibility. Then cross reference CRM data detailing how many captured leads and sales tie back to app origins to calculate accurate conversion rates.

Analyze what network relationships progress fastest from initial contact to the purchased customer and why. Which sale funnels performed smoothest to replicate? Does income generated outpace hourly participation costs? Essentially, gauge productivity in a multifactorial way - not just app vanity metrics like room entry applause. If desired business growth feels sluggish compared to the energy exerted, rework inefficient aspects. For example, time-block usage only during daily peak productivity hours instead of powering through evening fatigue chasing hype. Attend just the 3-5 rooms where ideal potential partners provably gather rather than sporadic random raids.

Or tighten follow-up activity by researching new members selectively to customize connection requests more meaningfully. Personalize emails recapping helpful dialogue while attaching free value-building resources.

With consistent review cycles determining what activities convert where the energy feels well invested versus wasted, social audio networking gets honed strategically. Measure and then tailor tactics to actual ROI beyond gut reactions. The numbers guide the next evolution.